D0522585

CONTENTS

Acknowledgements

We would like to thank Barry and Birgit Delamain-Blunt for the use of their home. Louise Woodridge, Katie O'Neill, Jacks Waters (Home Economist) Katharine Ibbs (Food Stylist) for their patience and hard work. John Roan Photography in Northampton for their inspired photography. Churchs China Store in Northampton for loaning us chinaware and props.
Published by Soutar Print in Northampton. © Lesley Waters 2003

apple and
walnut chutney

SERVES 4-6

115g butter

900g dessert apples, washed, cored and quartered

175g soft brown sugar
juice and zest of 1 lemon

2 tbsp brandy (optional)

225g walnut halves, roughly chopped

1. In a large saucepan, melt the butter and add the apples, sugar, lemon juice and zest.

2. Gently stir the ingredients to combine and cover with a lid. Cook the apples gently, over a low heat for 15-20 minutes or until just soft.

3. Remove the lid and turn the heat to high. Allow the chutney to cook uncovered, stirring occasionally, for a further 5-6 minutes or until most of the excess liquid has evaporated. Stir in the brandy (if using) and set to one side to cool.

4. When cool, stir in the walnuts and serve.

ingredients listed in green available from Julian Graves

walnut loaf

SERVES 6-8

225g strong white flour

225g malted granary flour

pinch of salt

1.5 teaspoons of quick yeast

150ml warm milk

1 egg, beaten

1 tbsp olive oil

150ml warm water

225g walnut halves

beaten egg to glaze

1. Sift the flours and salt into a large bowl. Stir in the yeast. Make a well in the centre of the flour and stir in the warm milk, beaten egg, olive oil and enough of the water to form a soft, wet dough.

2. On a lightly, floured surface, knead the dough for 10 minutes, until smooth and elastic.

3. Place the dough in a lightly oiled large bowl. Cover and leave to prove in a warm place for about 1 hour, until doubled in size.

4. When the dough has risen, knead it again to 'knock it back' and gradually incorporate the walnuts, until well distributed throughout the dough. Shape the dough into 1 large or 2 smaller rounds, as required. Place on a lightly floured baking sheet and slash the top of each loaf.

5. Preheat the oven to 220C/425F/Gas Mark 7.

ingredients listed in green available from Julian Graves

6. Cover the loaf (loaves) and return to a warm place until risen to approximately half their size again.

7. Glaze the loaves with beaten egg and bake in the oven for 10-15 minutes, then reduce the heat to 190C/375F/Gas Mark 5, and bake for a further 15 minutes for the smaller loaves or 30 minutes for the larger. The loaves are cooked when they are risen and golden and sound hollow when tapped underneath.

8. Cool on a wire rack.

peppered goat's cheese with fruit chutney

SERVES 4

2 tbsp olive oil

1 large onion, chopped

1/2 tsp ground ginger

1 tsp each of ground turmeric, coriander and cinnamon

225g dried whole pitted apricots, chopped

1 tbsp runny honey

juice and grated zest of 1 orange

300ml vegetable stock

2 tbsp sesame seeds, toasted

2 x 100g Somerset goat's cheeses

2 tbsp black peppercorns, smashed in a pestle and mortar

3 tbsp chopped fresh flat-leaf parsley

1. Preheat the oven to 200C/400F/Gas Mark 6.

2. In a wok or frying pan, heat the oil and gently fry the onion for 5 minutes until softened. Add the spices and gently fry for 30 seconds. Add the apricots, honey, orange juice and zest and vegetable stock. Simmer for 15-20 minutes. Stir in the sesame seeds.

3. Cut each goat's cheese in half and roll each in the cracked black pepper, pressing the pepper into the cheeses. Transfer to a baking tray, skin side down, and bake in the oven for 8-10 minutes.

4. To serve, stir the parsley through the chutney and serve at once with the hot peppered goat's cheese and some good crusty bread or mustard seed naans (see page 10).

ingredients listed in green available from Julian Graves

mustard seed naans

These instant naan breads are really great to serve with soups, curries, dhal or salads.

MAKES 4

225g self-raising flour

2 tbsp mustard seeds, dry-roasted

salt and freshly ground black pepper

150g natural yoghurt

25g butter, melted

1. Preheat the grill to a medium setting.

2. Place the flour in a bowl and mix in the mustard seeds, 1 tsp salt and plenty of black pepper. Stir in the yoghurt and mix well to form a soft dough.

3. Divide the dough into four and using your hands, press out each piece into a rough oval about 5mm thick.

4. Transfer to a non-stick baking tray dusted with a little flour and grill for about 3 minutes on each side until puffed and golden.

5. Brush each one with a little butter and serve at once.

ingredients listed in green available from Julian Graves

pumpkin seed, oat and raisin bread

This bread is excellent for dunking in soups or roughly torn and served with cheese.

SERVES 4-6

115g porridge oats

2 tsp baking powder

115g plain flour

115g raisins

2 tbsp roughly chopped fresh thyme

1 small onion, grated

1 egg

125ml milk

salt and freshly ground black pepper

3 tbsp olive oil

2 tbsp pumpkin seeds

1. Preheat the oven to 200C/400F/Gas Mark 6.

2. In a large bowl mix together all the ingredients, except the olive oil and pumpkin seeds, including 1 level tsp salt and plenty of pepper. The mixture will be quite wet, like a very thick batter.

3. Place a baking tray drizzled with 2 tbsp of the olive oil, in the oven and heat for 5 minutes. Spread the wet dough on to the hot baking tray and shape into a rough round, about15-18cm in diameter. Brush the remaining oil over the top and scatter over the pumpkin seeds.

4. Return to the oven for 20 min utes, then flip the bread over and continue to bake for a further 6-8 minutes or until brown.

5. Remove the bread from the oven and allow it to cool for a few minutes then cut it into wedges and serve warm.

ingredients listed in green available from Julian Graves

toasted almond & green bean salad

SERVES 4

100g blanched whole almonds, halved lengthwise

1 tsp olive oil

250g fine green beans, trimmed

200g char-grilled artichokes in olive oil, drained

8 baby plum tomatoes, halved squeeze of lemon juice

1 medium bag salad leaves

Moroccan harissa spice mill

extra virgin olive oil

1. Preheat the oven to 200C/400F/Gas Mark 6.

2. Toss the almonds in the olive oil and spread out on a baking tray. Roast in the oven for 10-12 minutes until lightly browned.

3. In a large pan of boiling water, cook the beans for 2 minutes until just tender.

4. Slice each artichoke into two to three bite-sized pieces and transfer to a large bowl. Add the tomatoes, lemon juice and salad leaves, toss together and divide between four serving plates.

5. Top each mound of salad with some warm beans. Grind a generous amount of Moroccan harissa spice over the hot almonds and scatter over the salad. Finish with a drizzle of extra virgin olive oil and serve at once.

pad thai **noodles**

SERVES 4

275g rice noodles

3 tbsp light soy sauce

2 tbsp fish sauce

2 tbsp sun-dried tomato paste

1 tsp sugar

3 tbsp sunflower oil

350g raw tiger prawns, peeled

2 cloves garlic, crushed

**2 hot red chillies, drained
de-seeded and finely chopped**

1 bunch spring onions, chopped

3 eggs, beaten

140g beansprouts

4 tbsp unsalted cashew nuts

**1 bunch fresh coriander, chopped
lime wedges to serve**

1. Cook the noodles as directed on the packet, drain, run under cold water and drain very well. Set to one side.

2. In a bowl, mix together the soy sauce, fish sauce, tomato paste, 3 tablespoons water and sugar. Set to one side.

3. In a large wok, heat the oil. Add the prawns and stir-fry for 1 minute. Add the garlic, chillies and spring onions and stir-fry for a further 2-3 minutes or until the prawns are just cooked.

4. Push the prawns, garlic, onions and chilli to the side of the pan, and pour the eggs into the empty side of the pan, over the heat. Cook the egg over the heat, stirring constantly for 1 minute or until the egg is just set.

ingredients listed in green available from Julian Graves

5. Mix all the pan contents together, pour in the soy sauce and tomato mix and heat gently. Add the beansprouts, rice noodles, cashew nuts and coriander. Toss everything together well and heat thoroughly.

6. To serve, pile the pad thai noodles into serving bowls and serve at once with the lime wedges.

seared tuna with sesame spinach

SERVES 4

4 x 150g fresh tuna steaks

4 tbsp olive oil

3 tbsp soy sauce

2 hot red chillies, drained de-seeded and finely chopped

salt and freshly ground black pepper

3 tbsp sesame seeds

2 tsp sesame oil

juice of 1/2 lime

250g baby spinach leaves, washed

225g halved baby plum tomatoes,

1. Place the tuna steaks into a shallow dish. In a bowl mix together 2 tbsp of the olive oil, 2 tbsp of the soy sauce and the chillies. Pour over the tuna steaks and season with freshly ground black pepper. Set to one side for 30 minutes.

2. Meanwhile, for the dressing, in a frying pan, dry-fry the sesame seeds over a medium heat for 1-2 minutes, stirring all the time until golden.

3. Tip the toasted sesame seeds into a small bowl. Add the remaining olive oil, soy sauce, the sesame oil and lime juice. Season to taste.

4. In a large mixing bowl, combine the spinach and tomatoes. Add the sesame dressing and toss well together.

ingredients listed in green available from Julian Graves

5. To serve, heat a non-stick griddle pan or large frying pan until really hot. Add the tuna steaks and any marinade and sear for just 1-2 minutes each side or until cooked to your liking.

6. Pile the spinach and sesame salad on to the middle of four serving plates and top each with the seared tuna steaks. Serve straightaway.

barbecue prawns with sesame and cucumber pickle

SERVES 4

16 extra large prawns, shell on

2 tbsp runny honey

2 tbsp olive oil

1 clove garlic, crushed
juice of 1/2 lemon

salt and freshly ground black
pepper

for the pickle

2 tbsp sesame seeds

150ml rice vinegar

4-5 tsp caster sugar

1 hot red chilli, drained
de-seeded and finely chopped

1 spring onion, finely chopped

1/4 cucumber, finely chopped

1. Put the whole prawns in a shallow dish. In a separate bowl mix together the honey, olive oil, garlic and lemon juice. Pour over the prawns, season with black pepper and set to one side for 30 minutes.

2. Place the sesame seeds in a dry pan over a medium heat. Toast until golden.

3. In a mixing bowl, combine the vinegar, sugar and chilli. Stir in the hot toasted sesame seeds, spring onions and cucumber. Season to taste and add extra sugar if required.

4. Remove the prawns from their marinade and lay directly on the barbecue grill. Cook for 1-2 minutes each side, until the prawns have turned pink and are lightly charred. Brush with the marinade from time to time. Remove from the heat and serve with the sesame and cucumber pickle.

ingredients listed in green available from Julian Graves

potato **rösti** with smoked trout and **orange** and **almond** vinaigrette

SERVES 4

3 large potatoes, peeled

salt and freshly ground black pepper

6 tbsp olive oil

1 tbsp wholegrain mustard

2 tsp white wine vinegar

2 tbsp fresh orange juice

25g flaked almonds, toasted

200g smoked trout

bunch of watercress, washed, trimmed

1. Grate the potatoes on the coarse side of a grater and dry really well on kitchen paper.

2. Put the grated potato into a bowl and season well with salt and freshly ground black pepper. Using your hands, divide the mix ture into four rounds.

3. Heat 2 tbsp of the olive oil in a large non-stick frying pan, add the potato rounds (you may need to do this in two batches). Flatten slightly with a fish slice and cook over a medium heat for 7-8 minutes each side until golden and cooked through.

4. Meanwhile make the dressing. Whisk together the mustard, vinegar, orange juice and remaining olive oil. Season well. Stir in the almonds.

5. Place each rösti on to a serving plate, and top with the smoked trout and watercress. Drizzle over the vinaigrette and serve straightaway.

morrocan fish pies

SERVES 4

4 spring onions, finely chopped

1 clove garlic, crushed

20 black olives, pitted and roughly chopped

2 tbsp chopped parsley

1 x 185g can tuna fish in oil, drained and flaked

1 tbsp olive oil

salt and freshly ground black pepper

8 large sheets filo pastry

25g butter, melted

4 medium eggs

1 tbsp poppy seeds

1 tbsp sesame seeds

to serve

baby salad leaves

1 lemon, cut into wedges

1. Preheat the oven to 200C/400F/Gas Mark 6.

2. In a bowl mix together the spring onions, garlic, olives, parsley, tuna and olive oil. Season well and set to one side.

3. Brush each filo sheet with melted butter and fold over in half. Trim each into a square approximately 20 x 20cm. Lay two squares of filo on top of each other and brush with butter. You now have a square consisting of four layers. Do the same with the other filo sheets, to make four squares.

4. Spoon the tuna mixture into the centre of each square then, using the back of a spoon, make a little dip to break an egg into each. Bring the four corners of the filo up towards the centre, covering the filling and forming a parcel.

ingredients listed in green available from Julian Graves

5. Using a fish slice, transfer on to a baking tray. Brush with butter and sprinkle over the seeds. Bake for 15 minutes until golden and crisp.

6. Serve hot with lightly dressed salad leaves and wedges of lemon.

mushroom and pine nut pizzas

SERVES 4

1 x 145g packet pizza base mix

2 tsp dried Provençal herbs

350g small field mushrooms, peeled, trimmed with the stalks left on

1 tbsp olive oil

For the onion parsley

1 medium red onion

2 tbsp chopped flat-leaf parsley

salt and freshly ground black pepper

for the garlic butter

55g butter, softened

1 clove garlic, crushed

to serve

4 tbsp pine nuts, toasted

100g rocket leaves

1. Preheat the oven to 220C/425F/Gas Mark 7.

2. In a large bowl, mix together the pizza base mix and herbs. Make up the pizza dough as directed on the packet, knead well and set to one side.

3. In a small food processor or blender make the onion parsley. Whizz together the red onion and parsley and season well. Set to one side.

4. Divide the dough into four and roll out each piece into a rough about 15cm round in diameter. Place on a baking tray and top each with some onion parsley, leaving a border around the out side. Crowd the mushrooms, stalk side up, on the top of the onion parsley.

ingredients listed in green available from Julian Graves

5. Brush the mushrooms and edges of the dough with a little olive oil and bake in the oven for 10-12 minutes until the bases are golden and crisp.

6. Meanwhile combine the butter and the crushed garlic and season.

7. Remove the mushroom pizzas from the oven and immediately top each mushroom stalk with a blob of garlic butter. Sprinkle with pine nuts. Top with rocket leaves and serve at once.

oriental chips with warm cashew dressing and crunchy salad

SERVES 4

for the chips
900g potatoes, peeled
3 tbsp olive oil
3 tbsp dark soy sauce
freshly ground black pepper

for the dressing
3 tbsp olive oil
200g cashew nuts
2 cloves garlic, crushed
2 tbsp dark soy sauce
juice of 2 limes
2 tbsp roughly chopped coriander

for the salad
140g beansprouts
115g watercress
2 carrots, peeled and cut into ribbons
2 tsp sunflower oil
1 tsp rice wine vinegar

1. Preheat the oven to 200C/400F/Gas Mark 6.

2. Cut the potatoes into very thick chips and place in a large, non-stick roasting tin. Pour over the oil and soy sauce and toss together. Season with black pepper.

3. Bake in the oven for 35-40 minutes, turning occasionally, until golden brown and crisp.

4. For the dressing, in a frying pan, heat the olive oil and fry the cashew nuts until golden. Add the garlic, soy sauce and lime juice (the pan will hiss dramatically). Remove from the heat and stir in 250ml water and the coriander. Set to one side to cool for a few minutes.

5. Meanwhile, place the beansprouts, watercress, and carrot ribbons in a bowl. Combine the sunflower oil with the rice wine vinegar and use to dress the salad ingredients, then arrange on a large serving plate.

ingredients listed in green available from Julian Graves

6. Transfer the cashew dressing to a liquidiser and whizz until smooth.

7. To serve, pile the cooked chips on top of the salad and spoon over some of the warm cashew dressing. Hand the remaining dressing separately and serve at once.

mediterranean
couscous

SERVES 4

2 red peppers, de-seeded

1 large aubergine

2 courgettes

1 large red onion, peeled

3 tbsp olive oil

salt and freshly ground black pepper

1 tbsp each of cumin and coriander seeds

115g fine green beans, trimmed

1 x 400g tin chickpeas, drained and rinsed

4 cloves garlic, crushed for the couscous

250g couscous

2 tbsp extra virgin olive oil

juice and zest of 1 lemon

large bunch coriander, roughly chopped

chilli oil to serve (optional)

1. Preheat the oven to 220C/425F/Gas Mark 7.

2. Prepare the peppers, aubergine and courgettes by cutting into chunks of about 4cm. Cut the onion into wedges. Place the prepared vegetables into a large roasting tin and toss with the olive oil. Season well.

3. Roast in the preheated oven for 25-30 minutes. Meanwhile roughly crush the cumin and coriander seeds in a pestle and mortar.

4. Add the green beans, chickpeas, garlic and ground spices to the vegetables and cook for a further 10-12 minutes.

ingredients listed in green available from Julian Graves

5. Meanwhile, place the couscous in a large bowl and cover with 300ml boiling water. Set aside for 5 minutes. Fluff up the cous cous with a fork, add the olive oil, lemon juice and zest and half the coriander. Toss well to evenly coat the couscous and season well.

6. To serve, spread the couscous out on a large serving dish. Pile the roasted vegetables on top and sprinkle over the remaining coriander. Finish with a drizzle of chilli oil.

lemon taglietelle with broccoli, broad beans and hazelnuts

SERVES 4

350g tagliatelle pasta

300ml double cream

juice and zest of 1 large lemon

salt and freshly ground black pepper

450g broccoli florets

200g podded broad beans, blanched and peeled

50g shelled hazelnuts, roasted and roughly chopped

1. Cook the tagliatelle pasta as directed on the packet.

2. Meanwhile, pour the cream into a pan and season with the lemon zest and juice, salt and lots of black pepper. Gently heat and simmer for 5 minutes.

3. Cook the broccoli in boiling water for 3 minutes. Add the broad beans and heat for a further 30 seconds. Drain well.

4. To serve, drain the pasta and return to the pan. Toss briefly with the lemon cream and pile into four serving bowls. Top with the broccoli florets and broad beans. Scatter over the hazel nuts and serve at once.

ingredients listed in green available from Julian Graves

savoury baguette pudding with avocado and pear salad

SERVES 4

25g butter, softened

1 small baguette, cut into 14 slices

100g Roquefort cheese, crumbled

50g mature Cheddar, grated

5 spring onions, finely chopped

1 tbsp blue poppy seeds

2 large eggs

250ml milk

salt and freshly ground black pepper

for the avocado and pear salad

5 tbsp olive oil

2 ripe dessert pears, halved, cored and sliced

1 large ripe avocado

1 tbsp lemon juice

25g walnuts halved (not shelled), toasted and roughly chopped

1 x 150g bag rocket salad

1. Preheat the oven to 190C/375F/Gas Mark 5.

2. Butter the slices of bread and arrange in an ovenproof serving dish. Scatter over the cheeses, spring onions and poppy seeds. Whisk together the eggs and milk and season well. Pour over the bread and set aside for 10 minutes.

3. Bake for 25-30 minutes until puffed and golden.

4. Meanwhile make the salad. Heat 2 tbsp of the oil in a griddle pan and cook the pears for 1 minute on each side until tender and golden but still holding their shape. Remove from the pan and set aside.

5. Halve, stone and peel the avocado, and cut into slices.

6. Whisk the remaining olive oil and lemon juice together. Season well and stir in the walnuts.

7. Arrange the griddled pear, avocado and rocket on a platter and drizzle over the dressing. Serve with the hot savoury baguette pudding.

Too much turmeric – not quite as I expected

dry -spice
aubergine oven curry

SERVES 4

2 tsp each of cumin and coriander seeds

6 cardamom pods

1 bay leaf

pinch of chilli powder

salt and freshly ground black pepper

2 medium aubergines, cut into approx. 2.5cm chunks

2 tbsp olive oil

1 x 400ml can coconut milk

1 x 410g can chickpeas, drained and rinsed

3 tbsp chopped fresh coriander

2 hot red chillies, drained de-seeded and finely chopped

1. Preheat the oven to 190C/375F/Gas Mark 5.

2. Using a pestle and mortar, blend together the cumin, coriander, cardamom, bay leaf, chilli powder and 1 tsp salt.

3. Place the aubergine in a roasting tin or ovenproof dish. Toss in the dry-spice mix and oil and season with black pepper.

4. Bake the aubergine in the oven for 25-30 minutes, or until the aubergine is lightly charred and tender.

5. Pour the coconut milk over the spiced aubergines, stir in the chickpeas and return to the oven for 15-20 minutes until bubbling hot.

6. Scatter over the coriander and chopped chilli and serve at once with warm naan bread or couscous.

ingredients listed in green available from Julian Graves

vegetarian

Too much turmeric — not quite as I expected.

bulgar pilaff with spiced peach and nuts

SERVES 4

250g bulgar wheat

1 tbsp sunflower oil

1 large onion, finely chopped

1 clove garlic, crushed

2 tsp each of ground turmeric and cumin

1 tsp ground coriander

1 cinnamon stick, split

115g dried peaches, chopped

115g raisins

1 bay leaf

2 large carrots, peeled and grated

600-850ml vegetable stock

salt and freshly ground black pepper

55g flaked almonds, toasted

2 tbsp roughly chopped fresh coriander

1 large lemon, cut into wedges

1. In a bowl, cover the bulgar wheat in boiling water for 15 minutes. Drain well.

2. Meanwhile, heat the oil in a large frying pan or wok and cook the onion for 5 minutes, until soft ened. Add the garlic, turmeric, cumin, coriander and cinnamon to the pan and cook for a further minute.

3. Add the fruits, bay leaf and car rots and pour in 450ml of the stock. Drain the bulgar wheat and add to the pan. Season well.

4. Cook the pilaff over a medium heat for a further 10-15 minutes, adding extra stock if necessary.

5. Spoon the pilaff into a large serving dish and stir in the almonds and coriander, reserving a tbsp of each to scatter over the top. Surround the pilaff with the lemon wedges and serve at once.

ingredients listed in green available from Julian Graves

griddled **chicken** with **aromatic** penne

SERVES 4

3 boneless, skinless chicken breasts

2 tbsp olive oil

juice of 1/2 lemon

salt and freshly ground black pepper

350g dried penne or any pasta of your choice

55g pine nuts, toasted

for the dressing

150ml olive oil

juice of 1 lemon

juice of 1 orange

1 tbsp ground cumin

125g dried apricots, chopped

1 bunch mint, chopped

1. Lay the chicken breast between two layers of non-pvc film, and using a rolling pin, bat out until about 5mm thick. Lay out in a non-metallic dish and pour over the olive oil and lemon juice. Season with black pepper and set to one side for an hour.

2. Cook the pasta as directed on the packet.

3. In a large bowl, mix together all the dressing ingredients. Drain the cooked pasta and toss with the dressing. Season well and set to one side.

4. To serve, heat a griddle pan until very hot. Sear the chicken breasts for 2-3 minutes each side until cooked, then cut up into rough strips. Pile the dressed pasta on to one large or four small serving dishes. Scatter over the griddled chicken and finish with the toasted pine nuts.

pork and pistachio kebabs with fresh tomato salsa

SERVES 4

450g minced pork

1 small onion, finely chopped

1 garlic clove, crushed

zest of 1 lemon

50g raw pistachio kernels, roughly chopped

salt and freshly ground black pepper

for the tomato salsa

1 large red pepper, de-seeded and finely diced

4 ripe tomatoes, diced

2 spring onions, finely chopped

1 clove garlic, crushed

pinch of sugar

squeeze of lemon juice

2 tbsp extra virgin olive oil

2 tsp Zulu fire spice

1. Soak eight wooden bamboo skewers.

2. In a bowl, mix together the minced pork, onion, garlic, lemon zest and pistachio nuts. Season well. Chill the mixture for 45 minutes.

3. Meanwhile, mix all the salsa ingredients together, and season to taste.

4. Preheat the grill to a medium setting.

5. Divide the pork mixture into eight and mould around the wooden skewers.

6. Grill the pork skewers on all sides for 15-20 minutes until golden and cooked through. Serve with the tomato salsa.

ingredients listed in green available from Julian Graves

cumin and mint lamb steaks with cucumber raita

SERVES 4

1 tbsp cumin seeds

1 tbsp black peppercorns

zest of 1 orange

3 tbsp fresh roughly chopped mint

4 x 150g leg lamb steaks

1 tbsp olive oil

for the cucumber raita

200g Greek yoghurt

1 clove garlic, crushed

1 tbsp coriander seeds, toasted and crushed

1/2 cucumber, peeled, de-seeded and coarsely grated

3 tbsp roughly chopped flat-leaf parsley

squeeze of lemon juice

1 tbsp olive oil

salt and freshly ground black pepper

1. Crush the cumin seeds and black pepper with a mortar and pestle. Add the orange zest and mint. Mix well.

2. Rub the lamb steaks with the olive oil and coat each side in the cumin and herb mixture.

3. Heat a griddle pan until really hot, add the lamb steaks and cook for 2-3 minutes on each side for rare or 4 minutes each side for medium, depending on thickness.

4. Whilst the lamb is cooking, mix together the yoghurt, garlic, coriander seeds, cucumber, parsley, lemon juice and olive oil. Season to taste.

5. Serve the steaks with the cucumber raita and some crisp green salad leaves.

ingredients listed in green available from Julian Graves

chicken fajitas with guacamole and tomato salsa

SERVES 4

4 boneless, skinless chicken breasts

for the spice rub
1 tbsp Hungarian paprika

1 tbsp each of cumin and coriander seeds, crushed

1/2 tsp salt

1 tsp caster sugar

1 tsp freshly ground black pepper

2 tbsp olive oil

to serve
8 flour tortillas, warmed

150ml soured cream

guacamole (see opposite)

tomato chilli salsa (see page 42)

1. Cut each chicken breast into five strips lengthways.

2. In a small bowl mix together the ingredients for the spiced rub. Add the chicken strips and toss together well to evenly coat. Cover, chill and leave for an hour to allow the spices to infuse the chicken.

3. Heat a griddle pan until hot. Add the chicken and griddle for 2-3 minutes on each side or until the chicken is cooked through.

4. Place the chicken on a large serving plate and hand around the tomato salsa, guacamole, soured cream and tortillas and allow your guests to assemble the fajitas themselves.

ingredients listed in green available from Julian Graves

quacamole

1 large ripe avocado, stoned, peeled and very finely diced
Juice of 1 lime
115g cherry tomatoes, diced
2 tsp tomato chutney
1 tbsp finely chopped onion
1 tbsp olive oil
2 tbsp roughly chopped fresh coriander (reserve a little for garnish)
1 hot red chilli, de-seeded and finely chopped
salt and freshly ground black pepper

1. Place the diced avocado in a bowl and squeeze over the lime juice.

2. Add all the remaining ingredients to the bowl, mix gently together
    and season with a little salt and lots of freshly ground black pepper.

sticky chilli beef with noodle salad

SERVES 4

4 hot red chillies, drained
de-seeded and finely chopped

2 tbsp runny honey

2 tbsp teriyaki marinade

1 tsp cumin seeds

2 tbsp sesame seeds

500g sirloin steak, cut into
thin strips

1 tbsp olive oil

for the noodle salad

250g egg noodles

3 carrots, peeled and cut
into ribbons

1/2 cucumber, peeled and cut
into ribbons

4 spring onions, finely chopped

1 small clove garlic, crushed

1 tbsp soy sauce

2 tbsp olive oil

2 tsp sesame oil

salt and freshly ground
black pepper

2 tbsp roughly chopped
fresh coriander

1. In a bowl mix together the
    chilles, honey, teriyaki marinade
    and cumin seeds. Add the beef
    and toss well to evenly coat. Set
    aside for 10 minutes.

2. Meanwhile, make the noodle
    salad. Cook the egg noodles as
    per packet instructions, drain
    and refresh.

3. Whisk the garlic, soy sauce, olive
    oil and sesame oil together.
    Season well.

ingredients listed in green available from Julian Graves

4. Toss the noodles, carrot ribbons, cucumber ribbons, spring onions and coriander with the dressing.

5. To cook the beef, heat the olive oil in a large wok. Toss the sesame seeds into the beef. Cook the beef in two batches over a very high heat for 2 minutes until just cooked, sticky and golden.

6. Serve the sticky, chilli beef with the noodle salad.

chicken and
cashew broth

SERVES 4

2 tbsp Madras curry paste

1 x 400ml can coconut milk

300ml vegetable stock

2 boneless, skinless chicken breasts, cut into thin strips

450g cauliflower florets

125g thread egg noodles

55g spinach washed, roughly shredded

100g cashew nuts, toasted

oil for deep-frying

1. Heat a wok or large pan. Add the curry paste and fry for 1 minute.

2. Add the coconut milk and stock and bring to the boil. Add the chicken and cauliflower florets to the broth and simmer for 8-10 minutes until just cooked.

3. Meanwhile cook the noodles as directed on the packet and drain.

4. Add the spinach to the broth and simmer for a further minute. Stir in the warm cashew nuts and season to taste.

5. Deep-fry the noodles, in two batches, in hot oil for 1-2 minutes, until golden and crisp.

6. To serve, ladle the broth into four bowls and top with crispy noodles. Serve at once.

chilli **chicken** with cashew sauce and honey-**glazed** pineapple

SERVES 4

4 boneless, skinless chicken breasts

2 cloves garlic, bashed

2 hot red chillies, drained de-seeded and chopped

juice and zest of 1 lime

juice of 1 orange

1 tsp light brown sugar

3 tbsp olive oil

1/2 small pineapple, core removed and cut into wedges with the skin on

1 tbsp runny honey

freshly ground black pepper for the cashew sauce

1/2 bunch spring onions, chopped

2 tbsp black bean sauce

juice of 1 orange

140g cashew nuts, toasted

4 tbsp roughly chopped fresh coriander

1. Lay the chicken breast between two layers of non-pvc film, and using a rolling pin, bat out until they are double their size. Using a sharp knife score each breast in a lattice fashion, taking care not to cut right through the flesh.

2. In a bowl, combine the garlic, chilli, lime juice and zest, orange juice, sugar and I tablespoon oil. Pour over the chicken and set to one side for at least 30 minutes.

3. Preheat the grill to its highest setting.

4. Heat 1 tablespoon of the olive oil in a large frying pan. Remove the garlic from the marinade, and lay in the chicken breasts scored side down in the pan, with all the marinade juices. Fry over a medium heat for 3-4 minutes each side or until the chicken is cooked.

ingredients listed in green available from Julian Graves

5. Meanwhile, brush the pineapple wedges lightly with honey and season well with black pepper. Grill for 6-8 minutes until lightly browned.

6. When the chicken is cooked, remove from the pan and set aside to keep warm. Add the remaining oil to the pan and fry the spring onions for 2-3 minutes until softened. Add the black bean sauce, orange juice and 150ml water and simmer for a further 2 minutes. Just before serving, stir in the cashew nuts and coriander.

7. Place each chicken breast on a large dinner plate. Spoon over some cashew sauce and garnish with the glazed pineapple. Serve with rice.

roast pork loin with fennel and roasted fruits

SERVES 4-6

1.5kg loin of pork, boned and rolled

1 tbsp olive oil

1 tbsp sea salt

3 tsp fennel seeds

for the roasted fruits

2 red onions, peeled and cut into wedges

2 tbsp olive oil

1 tsp brown sugar

salt and freshly ground black pepper

250g dried fruit selection (apricots, prunes, figs), roughly chopped

**300ml port
for the gravy**

2 tsp plain flour

100ml vegetable stock

250ml red wine

splash of balsamic vinegar

1. Preheat the oven to 220C/425F/Gas Mark 7. Score the pork skin vertically in thin strips with a very sharp knife (or ask the butcher to do this for you)!

2. Rub the skin with the olive oil, salt and fennel seeds. Place in a roasting tin and cook for 25 minutes to get the crackling going.

3. Reduce the oven to 190C/375F/Gas Mark 5. Cook for another 1 1/4 hours. (To roast pork, calculate 25 minutes per 450g, plus 25 minutes.)

4. Meanwhile, place the onions in a roasting tin and toss with the oil and sugar, Season well with salt and pepper and roast for 30 minutes. Add the fruit and port and return to the oven for 25-30 minutes. Season to taste.

5. Remove the pork from the roasting tin and place on a serving plate. Set aside and keep warm.

ingredients listed in green available from Julian Graves

6. To make the gravy, stir the flour into the tin, and cook over a medium heat for 1 minute. Gradually add the chicken stock and wine, scraping any sediment at the bottom and allow to simmer away for a few minutes. Add a splash of balsamic vinegar and season to taste.

7. Remove the crackling, carve the pork and serve with the roasted fruits. Hand the gravy round separately. Serve with crispy roast potatoes and vegetables of your choice.

Note:

To get really good crackling, leave the pork joint unwrapped in the fridge to let the skin dry. Also remember to take the joint out of the fridge at least 30 minutes before cooking so as to bring it up to room temperature.

citrus fruit tatin

SERVES 4-6

110g dried whole pitted apricots

110g dried figs, halved

110g pitted prunes

3 tbsp brandy

grated rind and juice of 1 orange

100g butter

100g demerara sugar

675g ripe pears, peeled, cored and thickly sliced

115g walnut halves

3 tsp sweet spice mix

3 tbsp caster sugar

300g ready-made shortcrust pastry

1. Preheat the oven to 200C/400F/Gas Mark 6.

2. In a bowl combine the dried fruits, brandy, orange rind and juice. Set to one side.

3. Heat the butter in a frying pan, add the sugar and cook until the sugar is melted and bubbling hot. Add the pears, dried fruits and their juices, and the walnuts and toss together. Turn into a non-stick 23cm spring- form tin or ovenproof round shallow dish.

4. Toss together the sweet spice mix and caster sugar and sprinkle onto a clean surface. Roll out the pastry into a 25cm round, in the sweet sugar spice mix. Lay the pastry on top of the pear mixture and press down gently.

5. Bake for about 35-40 minutes or until the pastry is cooked and the pears are just soft. Cool slightly in the tin, then invert onto a large serving plate to turn out. Best served warm with ice-cream.

ingredients listed in green available from Julian Graves

fruit and nut with brown sugar iced cream

SERVES 6

400ml double cream

400g Greek yoghurt

4 tbsp muscovado sugar

125g pecan nuts

4 tsp runny honey, gently warmed

125g blueberries

125g strawberries

1. In a large bowl, lightly whip the double cream. Fold in the yoghurt and transfer to a large shallow serving dish. Spread out with a palette knife and scatter the surface with the muscovado sugar. Transfer to the fridge for 2-3 hours or overnight.

2. To serve, preheat the oven to 200C/400F/Gas Mark 6. Scatter the pecan nuts on a baking tray and toast in the oven for 5 minutes. Remove and drizzle with the runny honey.

3. Place a large spoonful of muscovado iced cream on each serving plate with some warm honeyed pecans, blueberries and strawberries and serve at once.

Note:

For a very iced cream, transfer to the freezer for 30 minutes before serving.

ingredients listed in green available from Julian Graves

almond, plum and polenta cake

SERVES 6-8

1 unwaxed lemon, roughly chopped

225g butter

225g caster sugar

3 eggs

200g ground almonds

115g easy-cook polenta

1 tsp baking powder

8 plums, halved and stoned

15g demerara sugar

25g flaked almonds

icing sugar for dusting

1. Preheat the oven to 180C/350F/Gas Mark 4. Lightly grease a 26cm spring-form cake tin.

2. Place the roughly chopped lemon in a food processor and whizz until very chopped up.

3. Add the butter and caster sugar and whizz again.

4. Add the eggs, almonds, polenta and baking powder and whizz until well combined.

5. Turn the mixture into the tin and top with the plum halves, cut side down. Sprinkle over the demerara sugar and flaked almonds.

6. Bake in the oven for 1 hour, then reduce the heat to 160C/325F/Gas Mark 3, and bake for a further 15 minutes or until golden and firm to the touch.

7. Dust with a little icing sugar and serve warm with custard or vanilla ice- cream.

poppy seed and lemon muffins

MAKES 12

225g self-raising flour

2 tsp baking powder

225g unsalted butter, softened

4 large eggs

225g caster sugar

3 tbsp milk

2 tbsp blue poppy seeds

50g ground almonds

**2 lemons, zest only
(but reserve 2 tbsp lemon juice
for topping)**

for the topping

reserved lemon juice

150g mascarpone cheese

100g cream cheese

4 tbsp lemon curd

200g raspberries

1. Preheat the oven to 180C/350F/Gas Mark 4. Line twelve muffin moulds with paper cases.

2. Put the flour, baking powder, butter, eggs, sugar and milk in a food processor and mix well.

3. Add the poppy seeds, almonds and lemon zest and pulse the processor until mixed in well.

4. Spoon the mixture into the muffin cases, approximately half full. Bake for 20-25 minutes until just firm. Cool for 5 minutes, then remove to a cooling rack and leave to cool completely.

5. To make the topping, mix the lemon juice, mascarpone, cream cheese and lemon curd together. Spread over the top of the muffins and decorate with the raspberries.

ingredients listed in green available from Julian Graves

frangipane and warm honey tart

SERVES 8

1 x 375g pack ready-made
shortcrust or dessert pastry

little plain flour, for rolling

4 tbsp runny honey

for the frangipane

175g slightly salted
butter, softened

175g caster sugar

3 large eggs, beaten

150g ground almonds

55g plain flour

40g flaked almonds

to serve

4 tbsp clear honey

juice of 1/2 orange

Greek yoghurt

1. Roll out the pastry on a lightly floured surface and line the base and sides of a 28cm round loose-bottomed tart tin.

2. Spread the honey over the base of the pastry and set aside to chill.

3. Preheat the oven to 190C/375F/Gas Mark 5.

4. To make the frangipane, beat the butter and sugar together until pale and creamy. Gradually beat in the eggs. Stir in the ground almonds and flour then spread the mixture evenly over the pastry case. Scatter over the almonds.

5. Bake for 30-35 minutes until golden. Leave to cool for 10 minutes.

6. To serve, warm the honey and orange juice together in a small pan. Arrange a slice of tart on a serving plate. Drizzle over the warm honey syrup and serve with thick Greek yoghurt.

ingredients listed in green available from Julian Graves